55 EARTH
25 HOM

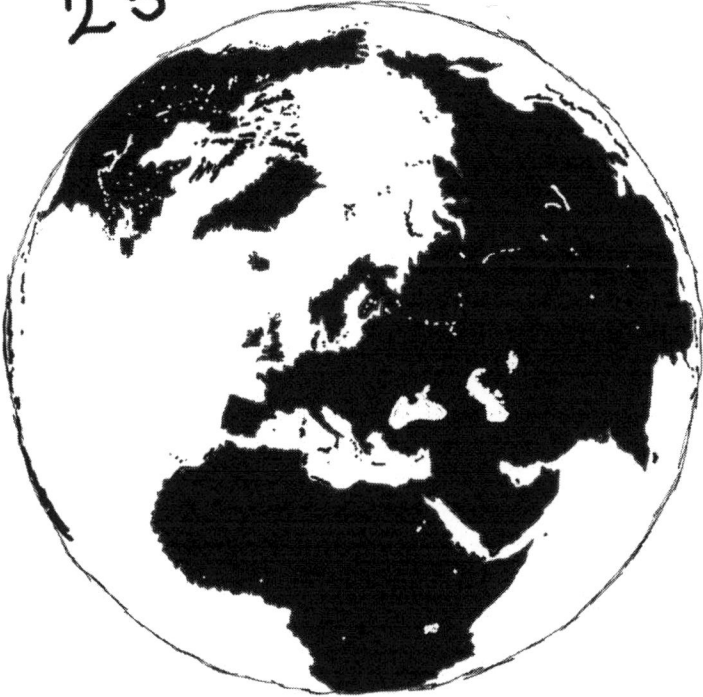

ADAM T. BURTON

ISBN 9781794528734

## DEDICATION

To all the home builders out there, making safe affordable homes. To my wonderful family and an extra special thank you to my amazing, funny, creative, supportive wife, Lilla.

xxxxxxxx
x

# HOME 1

23 CROCKFORD DRIVE
SUTTON COLDFIELD

THIS IS THE House that I was born in to in 1963. I was born at about 4 O'clock in the afternoon. My sister had Just arrived home from School.

# HOME 2

217 Litchfield Road
Four Oaks.
THE MOST AMAZing thing happened while I
was living in this house. IN July 1969 THE First
HUMAN EXPLORERS LANDED ON
the Moon. I WAS 6 years old
when I looked UP At the Moon
I knew.
People
were
there.

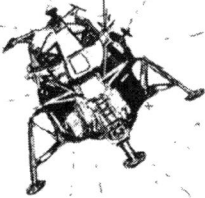

And this was
thrilling.

# HOME 3

177 COURT LANE
ERDINGTON

MY BROTHER. SIMONS AUSTIN HEALY SPRITE. IT WAS BLUE AND FAST AND FUN

AS I HAD A BIRTHDAY COMING UP I THOUGHT IT A good IDEA TO REMIND MY FAMILY By WRITING THE DETAILS ON THE NEW PIANO KEYS

8TH MAY BIRTH DAY.

178 LÔN GWERN

IN 1973 WE MOVED to NEWTOWN in mid wales. we stayed with my AUNTY MARGARET for a while IN TREHAFREN. At school they realised that I couldn't see and needed glasses... I WAS horrified. I WAS 10.

But at Least I could now See.....

The house was so cold at Night that Aunty Margaret Knitted us all brightly coloured bed socks.

# HOME 5

1 OAKFIELD TERRACE, NEWTOWN

MY MUM AND STEP DAD started a TAXI BUSINESS They had 2 LONDON Cabs and an AUSTIN 1800

MY Friend From BRUM, TASHI would Come and Stay. ONCE There was a TERRIFIC STORM, we Borrowed ONE OF MY MUMS SHeets

AND we took OFF, we FLEW. BAD Boys!

# HOME 6

## 362 LON EITHIN TREHAFREN
### NEWTOWN

Running a TAXI Business Took a great toll on my Mum and Step Dad, eventually they closed the business and sold the house. We were in Line for our own Trehafren house, but would have to wait. We moved in with my sister. My Mum and stepDAD would have the spare room, my stepbrother had joined the Parachute regiment. And I slept in the Cupbourd under the stairs. I Loved it.

# HOME 7

257 LÔN PINWYDD, TREHAFREN NEWTOWN.
I LOVED THIS HOUSE. I Had a big BEDroom to myself.
I would watch Movies on TV
from the 1940s. I Loved HITCHCOCK
Kubrick, WELLS, HOUSTAN, RENE
Clair. AND would go to the CINEMA
Whenever I could.

I MADE A MOSS GARDEN for
My MUM for MOTHERS Day
I went down the river and
collected Mud and twigs and
Moss and            STONES
I think
she liked
it.
♡

Our
ITT
COLOUR
TELLY

Alfred Hitchcock

# HOME 8

## THE WIESS HOUSE, LAKELAND FLA. USA.

WHEN I WAS 15 I TRAVELLED WiTH MY 81 YEAR OLD FRIEND GRANDMA BIC to the STATES. WE FLEW ON FREDDIE LAKER'S SKYTRAIN TO A DIRTY AND SEEDY PRE GIULIANI NEW YORK CITY. NEXT WE flew TO TAMPA, WE WENT our separate ways. I WENT to School in LAKELAND, Staying with the WIESS FAMILY. IT WAS A huge culture shock, but fascinating to me. THE MOST confusing thing to me was how very religious People were. The US was the richest country in the world in 1979. So much was available, I had my first McDonald's. And stood out Like a sore thumb at school. I got terribly homesick, I missed my mum and my family, we sent letters and cassettes.

Single TICKET TO NEW York £59

POLK COUNTY SCHOOL BUS

# HOME 7: RETURNED

257 LÔN PINWYDD, TREHAFREN NEWTOWN

I SPENT the Next 3 years teaching myself everything I could about film and Photography. I turned my

SUPER 8 CANON

NIKON F3

Bedroom into a darkroom, I photographed everything.

I eventually got a Technician.

Job in MONTGOMERY as a silk screen and NEWTOWN.

I Left the Job scared that I would Live there forever.

# HOME 9

**6 CREST COURT, BOBBLESTOCK, HEREFORD**
A horrible place to Live, in the suburbs of
HEREFORD. I was very Lonely, Jobless and homesick.
I DID however Learn that I could turn Just
about any space into a Darkroom.

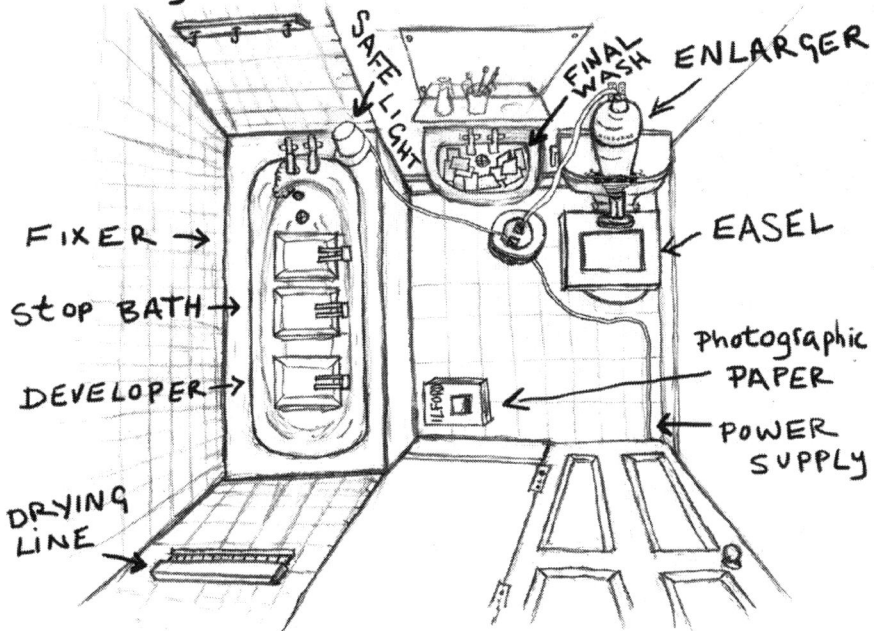

SAFE LIGHT

FINAL WASH

ENLARGER

FIXER →

Stop BATH →

DEVELOPER →

← EASEL

Photographic
PAPER

POWER
SUPPLY

DRYING
LINE →

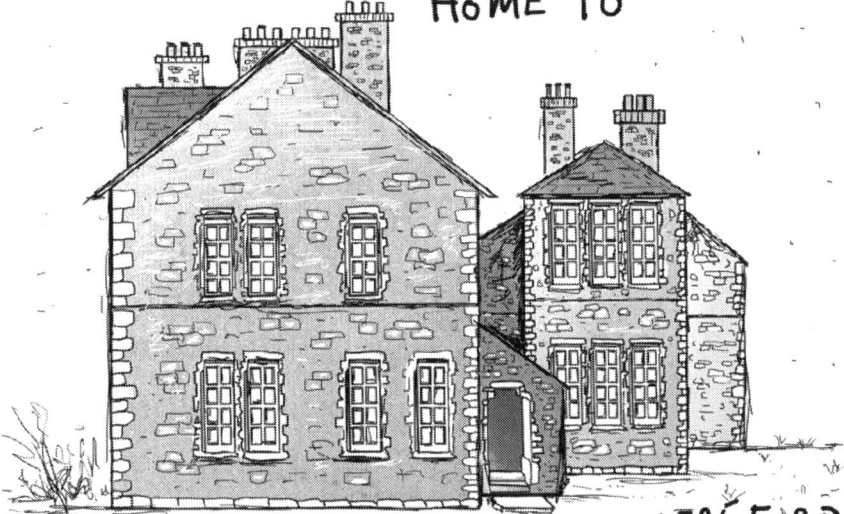

## THISTLEDEAN, CLEHONGER, HEREFORD

During the short time I Lived in this hotel on the outskirts of Hereford MY STEPDAD JIM, DIED. He Had a Heart attack while being operated on for stomach Cancer. Jim Advised Me to Punch the bully who had been Picking on Me at school. He was an excellent driving instructor and taught me to drive and would Laugh until he cried at "it's a knockout." I left this place to be with My MuM. when I returned to Hereford I MoveD INTO A New HOME. ♡

# STRATFORD HOUSE, HEREFORD

Built for the homsick wife of a victorian industrialist Stratford house was full of references to Shakespear's sonnet's and plays. even the front resembled the Globe theatre. I Paid £18 a week for a wonderful room in the eves.

I Loved Living in Bedsits commercial travellers were still Living in these places then. Sadly this form of Living is now gone. converted to flats.

1930s Baby Belling Cooker

cold TAP

A divorced Journalist for the local Paper Lived down the Hall. Her daughter was a fashion student in London.

THE Perfect Bedsit kitchen.

# HOME 12

HILL HOUSE, HEREFORD
MY LANDLORD ASKED me if I MINDED MOVING out OF STRATFORD House AND MOVE INTO ANOTHER OF HIS Houses. I DIDN'T WANT to but DIDN'T really have A choice. TURNED OUT to be quite a good MOVE. My MUM Came over from NEWTOWN to drive the hire VAN (I was too young). There was a separate kitchen which made a great DARKROOM. THE Main room WAS Huge and it had a gas FIRE with a 50p METER. on the WALL NEXT TO THE WINDOW was a CONTRAPTION THAT would gently

Drop you to the ground IN the EVENT OF A FIRE. TASHi came to visit ME here Just before he went off to become A MONK.

# HOME 13

## 138 JOHN NASH CRESCENT, HULME, MANCHESTER

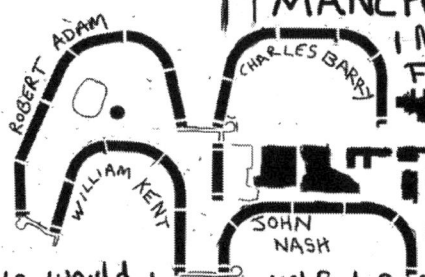

I MOVED TO THIS 4 Bedroom FLAT IN 1984. I Heard David BOWIE Perform at MAINE ROAD IN 1987. I got the most wonderful cat, MILOU from Tibb street.

ROBERT ADAM
CHARLES BARRY
WILLIAM KENT
JOHN NASH

He would be a faithful friend for 20 years. I met another faithful friend at this time, on a video course at the Collage of adult education. The very talented and creative MICK CONEFREY. WE MADE VIDEOS For bands. He has always Looked out for me and I have worked for and with him on TV shows and iLLuSTRATED HIS BOOKS. I will be for ever grateful to my smartest friend.

I DID A Drama course with RUDY GOLD

# HOME 14

GWEL-Y-DON (see the wave) ABERARTH
I RENTED THIS HOUSE from my friend NEVILLE JONES
From the outside toilet roof at the end of the garden
I could sit with Milou and watch Lightning storms
out to sea. My friend ALAN RADDON Lives across the
river, He is an artist, shoemaker, advertising man and free
thinker and a hippy. We had
MANY great ADVENTURES.

**A**

## CARAVAN, GWARLLYN, PENUWCH.

I moved from sea level to 600 FT up and 7 miles INLAND. THE caravan was falling to bits, and damp until I installed this fabulous 1954 RAYBURN room Heater, with the help of ANDY and ROB. Suddenly it became the coziest place on the planet in the WINTER OF 1989. Milou and I would go into the forest and trim and drag out fallen trees, some as large as thirty feet and chop them down to fit in the stove. I burnt it unseasoned so my chimney which was CAST IRON would get coated with RESIN and would very often catch fire and look like a flame thrower.

# HOME 16

## 3 QUEENS RD ABERYSTWYTH

I Rented A Room in the Carr's house. Jenny Bought this Large house with the plan to rent out rooms to students. Her four teenage children Lived with her. TESSA, HOWARD, Susi and Fred And their dog TOSH. THE TENANTS WERE Andy, PhiL, GITAM, Judith and me and MiLOU. It was a BIT of a MAD house, but Lots of Fun. Phil and howard and I Put on an event at the university students union "SWANK" WE D.J.ed and had gogo Dancers on pLinths (male and female) A few years Later Phil Started Clwb 23. for Such a SMall town Aber had a Lot going on. Aber Suited Me well. AND it was great to be Living by the Sea again. Phil introduced Me to his friend Loretta at a training place and I went on a word processing course and Started writing FiLM Scripts.

# HOME 17

# EVERTON 7 CLIFF TERRACE, ABERYSTWYTH

THIS was a great little Flat. £50 a week, it even had a garden cut into the cliff. I started writing with Dan Davies and had Many happy hours in stitches at the antics of our characters. I was shooting FILM for first TIME Directors, even helped to win the D.M. Davies award at the welsh international Film festival. When I moved out, My Friend MATT Moved in, and when he moved out our Friend BUZZ Moved iN.

# HOME 18

## 135 NORTHVIEW RD, HORNSEY, LONDON

ARRIFLEX BL
INTRODUCED in 1965.
MY DREAM CAMERA

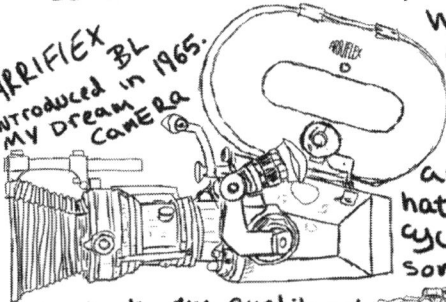

WHAT A DISASTROUS choice this move was for me. I NEVER GOT ON with LONDON. IT WAS too wealthy, too expensive and too busy for me. I hated public transport so cycled everywhere. I DID some interesting bits of life suffered.

work, but my quality of I DID however get to be very proficient with my all time favorite camera.

THE 16MM ARRI BL.
A wonderful
sound sync
MOVIE Camera.
RENTED, Not owned.

MY RALEIGH LIZARD

LONDON KILLS
ME: HANIF KUREISHI

41

## THE TARDIS, 555 MI SOL, TORREVIEJA, SPAIN

IN the year of my MUMS 70th birthday I got to live in Spain. I had only briefly seen my mum once or twice a year when she moved out there. It was the first time in Many, Many years that Mum and Simon and Sally and Me were all in the same place. When my mum moved there and built her own house she built a self contained annex which we called the Tardis. It looked Tiny on the outside but spread out on the inside because of the wedge shaped Plot. We all Lived there at some point over the years. The only problem was that I couldn't take Milou, he stayed with ENID, but I DID phone him regularly. When I got back to the UK. he remembered me.

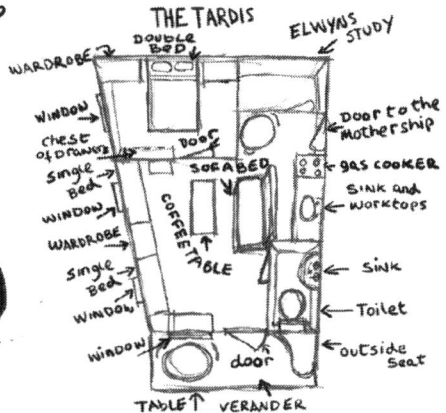

MiiiLOOOO

MAOW

### THE TARDIS

ELWYNS STUDY

WARDROBE
DOUBLE BED
WINDOW
CHEST OF DRAWERS
DOOR
Door to the mothership
SINGLE BED
SOFABED
gas COOKER
WINDOW
SINK and WORKTOPS
WARDROBE
COFFEE TABLE
SINGLE BED
SINK
WINDOW
Toilet
WINDOW
door
outside Seat
TABLE
VERANDER

MR DIY BLOKE    THE JOLLY FRIER

FLAT, LIMETREE AVENUE, WYMONDHAM

A VERY cheap FLAT £35 a week, in fact the owners
said it could be bought for £13,000. It
had no heating so was Damp and expensive
running electric fires, but it was a Roof.
Bought a wreck of a boat, plywood,
18 ft long with sails and a mast. £135
I spent 3 months replacing the Rotten
wood and painting and getting it ready
for Launch. 'Khrysta' sailed terribly
but was a great escape from the flat.
She was moored at Coltishall, Norfolk Mead
HOTEL.

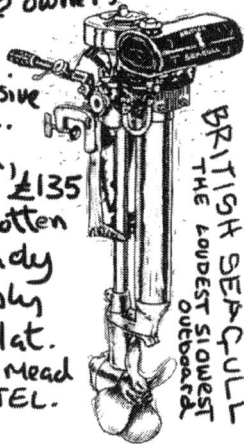

BRITISH SEAGULL
THE LOUDEST SLOWEST OUTBOARD

'Khrysta'

## KESTREL, BRUNDALL, NORFOLK

THIS was a 32FT Timber broads Cruiser, 7½ TONS. MY home for 13 years. I did a bit of work in the boatyards which was useful to Learn about Maintainance. IN THE end the boat became beyond repair, it was built In 1957 of Mahogany, not great in Fresh water. It turns to compost. for 15 years I replaced planks, but you have to know when to give up. It Cost me £1000 to demolish the boat and have the bite sized bits taken away in skips. I cut it up With a Jig Saw and a crow bar, it was a horrible experience.

on boxing Day 2004, the day the Tsunami happened Milou had a stroke, he had been a great companion for 20 years.

While living on this boat Nick and Loretta gave me a Laptop with Photoshop on it to encourage me to make art. This Led me on a whole New Path.

HOME 22

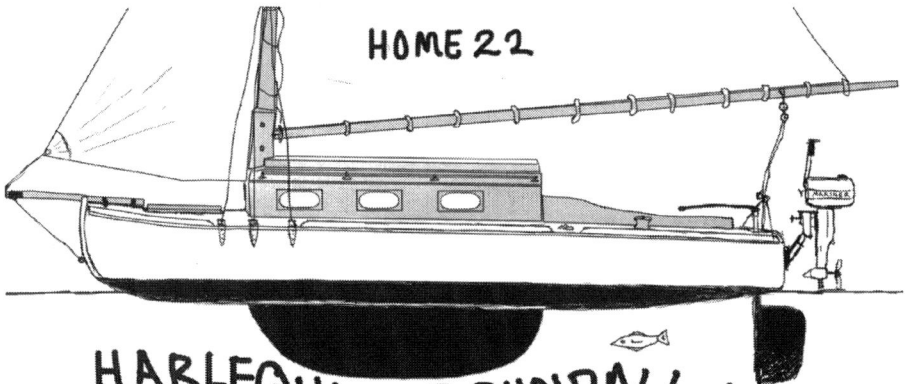

# HARLEQUIN, BRUNDALL, NORFOLK

AFTER chopping up Kestrel I had to live on harlequin, A 1953 broads Sailing Yacht, 24Ft Long, Made of Pitch pine and Mahogany not in the best Condition. IN fact the next owners abandoned her restoration. The only headroom came from a lifting tent roof, I Cooked in the tented Cockpit and used the boat yards bathroom.

I finally fulfilled an ambition during this time of starting my Degree course at university, first on the Photography Course and then transferring to the fiNE ART Course. Where I achieved a first class HONOURS.

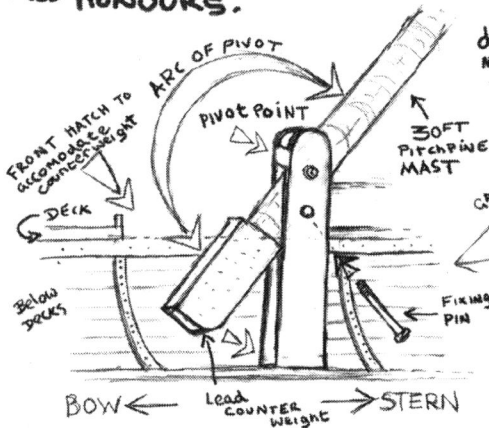

HARLEQUIN had a very well designed Counterweighted Lifting Mast which could be operated by one person from the bow Deck.

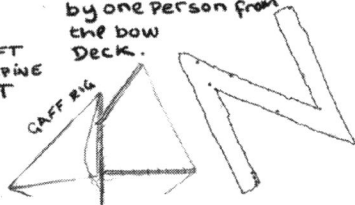

FRONT HATCH TO accommodate counterweight

ARC OF PIVOT

PIVOT POINT

30FT Pitchpine MAST

GAFF RIG

DECK

Below Decks

FIXING PIN

BOW ←    Lead COUNTER WEIGHT    → STERN

**NORWICH UNIVERSITY OF THE ARTS**

49

HOME 23

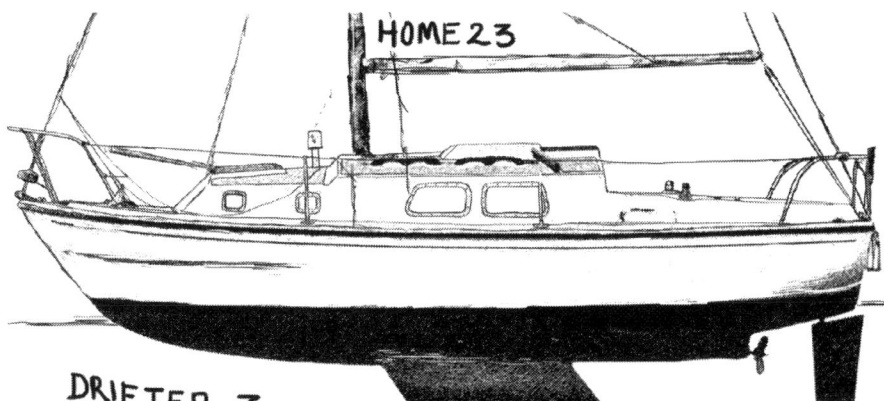

# DRIFTER 3, BRUNDALL, NORFOLK

THIS WAS by Far the best Live aboard situation. DRifter Was a westerly centaur, 26FT INBoard YANMAR Diesel engine and Made of Fiberglass in 1979. The Perfect size and space. She was solid and strong and sailed and Motored well. Sometimes at my mooring in Brundall the tide would go out so much I would be left high and Dry. I would wake up and everything would be at a strange funhouse Jaunty Angle.

I Fitted a Taylor's Drip Feed Diesel cabin heater which Pumped out 4KW of heat, it was very cosy.

Such a great boat and a great home.

# HOME 24

## OLD LAUNDRY COURT, NORWICH

My very good friend Simon came up trumps and let me live in one of his rooms for a while when I needed it most. It was a lot of fun living with Simon. Lilla would bring Irma, her dog over and stay with me at the weekends. When Lilla and I did the legal bit of our wedding Simon was our witness.

## CAMBRIDGE STREET, NORWICH

This cute little Terrace house was built in 1860, originally a 2 up 2 Down with a cold tap in the Kitchen. Many changes have made this the perfect house for us, with many more rooms and extended Kitchen. I have learnt, as you can see, that spaces can have multiple uses, that still holds true, our bathrooms become darkrooms, our bedroom doubles up as a recording studio, the Kitchen is also a textile studio with Lilla's wool carding, spinning and weaving

Lilla Molho

Where to Next?

Who Knows?

ADAM T BURTON Received a
FIRST CLASS HONS Degree in FINE
ART FROM NORWICH UNIVERSITY OF
THE ARTS.


More work on
adamtburton.wixsite/dirtyFILthyFiLM

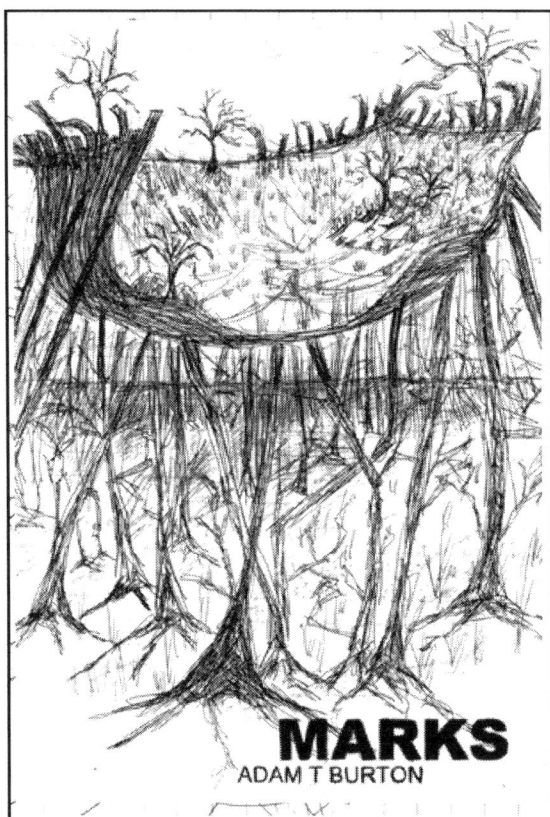

**MARKS**
ADAM T BURTON

also available by
ADAMT BURTON
MARKS

Printed in Great Britain
by Amazon

47973177R00035